SELECTIONS BY JOSHUA PRAGER

100 YEARS

VISUALIZATIONS BY MILTON GLASER

WISDOM FROM FAMOUS WRITERS
ON EVERY YEAR OF YOUR LIFE

W. W. Norton & Company
Independent Publishers Since 1923
New York · London

Excerpt from *Slapstick: A Novel* by Kurt Vonnegut. By permission of The Trust
Under the Will of Kurt Vonnegut, Jr.
"Men at Forty" from *Collected Poems* by Donald Justice, copyright © 2004 by Donald
Justice. Used by permission of Alfred A. Knopf, an imprint of the Knopf Doubleday
Publishing Group, a division of Penguin Random House LLC. All rights reserved. Used
by permission of Anvil Press Poetry for UK/Commonwealth from *Collected Poems* by
Donald Justice, copyright © 2006.
Claudia Rankine, excerpt from *Don't Let Me Be Lonely: An American Lyric*. Copyright © 2004
by Claudia Rankine. Reprinted with the permission of The Permissions Company, Inc.,
on behalf of Graywolf Press, www.graywolfpress.org.
"who are you, little i." Copyright © 1963, 1991 by the Trustees for the E. E. Cummings
Trust, from *Complete Poems: 1904–1962* by E. E. Cummings, edited by George J. Firmage
Used by permission of Liveright Publishing Corporation.
"Passing Through." Copyright © 1985 by Stanley Kunitz, from *The Collected Poems* by
Stanley Kunitz. Used by permission of W. W. Norton & Company, Inc.
Nazim Hikmet, excerpt from "On Living," translated by Randy Blasing and Mutlu
Konuk, from *Poems of Nazim Hikmet*. Copyright © 1994, 2002 by Randy Blasing and
Mutlu Konuk. Reprinted by permission of Persea Books, Inc (New York),
www.perseabooks.com. All rights reserved. Used by permission of Kalem Agency.

For information about permission to reproduce selections from this book, write to
Permissions, W. W. Norton & Company, Inc.,
500 Fifth Avenue, New York, NY 10110

For information about special discounts for bulk purchases, please contact W. W. Norton
Special Sales at specialsales@wwnorton.com or 800-233-4830

Manufacturing through Asia Pacific
Book design by Milton Glaser
Production manager: Louise Mattarelliano

Library of Congress Cataloging-in-Publication Data

100 years : wisdom from famous writers on every year of your life / selections by Joshua
Prager ; visualizations by Milton Glaser.—First edition.
     pages cm
ISBN 978-0-393-28570-3 (hardcover)
1. Life—Quotations, maxims, etc. 2. Aging—Quotations, maxims, etc. 3. Authors—
Quotations, maxims, etc. 4. Literature—Quotations, maxims, etc. 5. Conduct of life—
Quotations, maxims, etc. I. Prager, Joshua. II. Glaser, Milton. III. Title: One hundred years.
PN6084.L53A16 2016
082—dc23
                                2015029530

W. W. Norton & Company, Inc.
500 Fifth Avenue, New York, N.Y. 10110
www.wwnorton.com

W. W. Norton & Company Ltd.
15 Carlisle Street, London W1D 3BS

3 4 5 6 7 8 9 0

TO HILDA AND
MAX PRAGER,
MY BABA
AND PAPA,
WHO LIVED A
COMBINED
186 YEARS AND
HELD TIGHT
TO EVERY ONE
OF THEM.

Joshua Prager

TO
ELEANOR
EUGENE
ESTELLE
IRVING
JIVAN
GIORGIO
JEAN MICHELE
AND SHIRLEY
FELLOW PASSENGERS

Milton Glaser

LIFE PASSES INTO PAGES
IF IT PASSES INTO ANYTHING

James Salter, *Burning the Days*

Six years ago, in successive months, I read something Louis Menand wrote about being nineteen, and Don DeLillo wrote about twenty.

"We thought that discovering a new poet or a new poem was the most exciting thing in the world," Menand wrote in *The New Yorker* magazine. "When you are nineteen years old, it can be." Wrote DeLillo in his novel *Libra*: "At twenty years old, all you know is that you're twenty. Everything else is a mist that swirls around this fact."

I was thirty-eight and prone to meditating on age and time; an illness in the family (and later an injury to me) had long made clear that one could not assume that one would grow old.

But books offer vicarious experience. As James Salter wrote: "Life passes into pages if it passes into anything." And upon reading Menand and DeLillo, a thought leapt to mind: somewhere observations were written of *every* age. If I could find them, I could assemble them into a long life — and experience it too.

The thought had lingered in me for years when I saw a movie called *The Clock*. In it, hundreds of snippets from previous films showing clocks were spliced together so that every minute of the day ticked by. The film was magical and propulsive and spoke of time. My list would too, I hoped. And so, I decided to assemble it — passages for every age from zero to one hundred.

————

I sent a note to bookish friends but got no worthy suggestions back. I had three students browse concordances but had no luck there, either. Emailing author societies and a literary list-serve landed me a few passages but also got me scorned as illiterate. Progress was slow; when I then read novels by Thomas

Mann and Leo Tolstoy, I found two passages in 2700 pages.

So I began trolling Google Books and Amazon, searching pages and pages for ages and ages. I was soon seeing authors anew, wondering only if they were apt to reflect upon a specific age. Some, like Evelyn Waugh and Martin Amis, did so often. Some rarely did — it was only in an aside in his forgotten *Israel Potter* that Herman Melville, my literary hero, made the list. Some never did: Agatha Christie and Upton Sinclair each wrote more than 80 books but not one sentence I found that met my criteria.

Those criteria were simple. A passage had to explicitly state an age and convey something *about* it.

I was mindful that any such insights were relative. For starters, we now live longer and so age more slowly. (Christopher Isherwood used the phrase "the yellow leaf" to describe a man of fifty-three one century after Lord Byron used it to describe himself at thirty-six.)

But even so, as the list coalesced, the

great sequence of life revealed itself, as distinct as the stages that psychologist Jean Piaget observed of the very young. Here were the wonders and confinements of childhood, the emancipations and frustrations of adolescence, the empowerments and millstones of adulthood, the recognitions and resignations of old age. There were patterns to life. And they were shared. As Mann wrote of human experience: "It will happen to me as to them."

As such, those who did not make the list were usually in concert with their counterparts who did. Friedrich Von Trapp, independent and self-assured and transported at fourteen by the sound of music, resembled Anne Frank who wrote at fourteen in her diary. The consul whom Graham Greene wrote wished to stay put at sixty-one would identify with Robinson Crusoe whom Daniel Defoe observed at that same age.

Of course, life can swing unpredictably from year to year. Arthur Rimbaud distilled carefree seventeen in the time

Charlotte Brontë was first clearing her throat about the gravity of eighteen. And people may experience the same age differently. P. G. Wodehouse linked fifty-five to suicide while Fyodor Dostoevsky saw in it real and true enjoyment. Where Mann wrote of fulfillment at age thirty, F. Scott Fitzgerald saw in it diminishment.

Other discrepancies owed, perhaps, to gender. Maya Angelou learned surrender at fifteen, the same age of the boy who longed, wrote Günter Grass, "to enter a fray." And Nora Ephron and Norman Mailer saw in forty-three and forty-four opposing physical truths.

I am now forty-four. And I have a better sense of what awaits. For the list is complete. Thirty (Fitzgerald) was the first in place. Seventy (Nâzım Hikmet) was the last. The teens came together as quickly as they pass. The nineties were as difficult to compile as I imagine they are to live. Four was fallow, thirty-four fertile — William Wordsworth and Henry Thoreau, Ernest Hemingway and Haruki Murakami, all moved to write. The beginnings of decades inspired many pens, so each got an extra passage.

A note — I used quotation marks only when the passage was dialogue. Those few passages containing ellipses were pruned not with their original context in mind but this one, mindful only that they speak to the age in question. I allowed just one passage per writer. And, of course, I only harvested a tiny patch of the written word.

Like life, the list is circuitous. And like the spin of a globe, its compiling sent me into distant lands — from Persepolis to Tara to Oz. Always, I was happily lost, forgetting why I was where I was, remembering only to read.

May you get *happily* lost too. And, in the words of Hikmet, may "you know that living is the most real, the most beautiful thing."

Joshua Prager
New York City
July 2015

WORDS, COLOR, AND TIME

When Joshua Prager first called me
after seeing some clocks I had designed
for the Museum of Modern Art, he
wondered if I might be interested in
designing a clock that took 120 years
to complete one revolution. Truthfully,
I had no idea what he was talking
about. But we got to talking about time.
He then told me that he'd collected a
series of quotations for every year in an
individual's life and would like to send
them to me for my opinion. The idea
seemed simple enough, but the quality
and appropriateness of the quotations
was overwhelming.

One of the reasons I'd found the
selections particularly provocative
might have been the fact that a few

weeks earlier I had begun cleaning out my library in preparation for a move. I was trying to separate those books that remained essential to my life from those that would languish on a shelf, read or unread, forever. I discarded the less meaningful from the essential ones at a ratio of 10 to 1. It saddened me to think of giving them away, but I suddenly had the realization that almost everyone on earth has the same problem. The great books we've read live largely in our memory (mine is rapidly disappearing).

The intersection of words and form has always been central to my work as a designer. Words create narrative, but the visual world speaks to us in another way. The pleasure of viewing a painting or sculpture can persist for a lifetime of repeated viewings. Of course, all books are designed, with trim size, typography, margins, each created to support the literary objectives and make the subject understandable. In most works of graphic design the typography is chosen to express or amplify the author's tone or spirit.

In the case of *100 Years*, I wanted to have the reader/viewer *experience* the book rather than understand it. The annual passage of time is represented by the blended changing of color that runs horizontally through the book. Daily life, including dates of birth, seems to move vertically, and each page in the book also blends in color from top to bottom. The number changes style from page to page, creating a mutable relationship between the words and the color.

What I'm hoping for in *100 Years* is a work that changes every time you look at it depending on the context; lying open on a table, read in poor light, read in good light, read front to back, sideways or upside down. Some years ago, I wrote a book entitled *In Search of the Miraculous or One Thing Leads to Another*. It dealt with the idea that all things are in some way invisibly connected. With this little book you are now holding in your hand we are hoping that, through the simplest means — paper, ink and type — something unpredictable will happen.

Milton Glaser
New York City
July 2015   *

Birth was the
death of him.

Samuel Beckett,
A Piece of Monologue

BIRTH

I was slapped and hurried
along in the private applause of
birth…. the fantastic sloppiness
of one's coming into existence,
one's early election, one's senses
in the radiant and raw stuff of
howlingly sore and unexplained
registry in the new everywhere,
immensely unknown, disbelief
and shakenness, the awful
contamination of actual light.
I think I remember the breath
crouched in me and then leaping
out yowlingly: this uncancellable
sort of beginning.

Harold Brodkey, *The Runaway Soul*

1

At <u>one</u> year of age the child says
his first *intentional* word…. And,
just here, a great war springs up
within him. It is the struggle
of consciousness against the
machine. This is the first conflict
in man, the first warfare between
his parts!

Maria Montessori,
The Absorbent Mind

2

One day when she was <u>two</u>
years old she was playing in a
garden, and she plucked another
flower and ran with it to her
mother. I suppose she must have
looked rather delightful, for
Mrs. Darling put her hand to
her heart and cried, "Oh, why
can't you remain like this for
ever!" This was all that passed
between them on the subject, but
henceforth Wendy knew that
she must grow up. You always
know after you are two. Two
is the beginning of the end.

J. M. Barrie, *Peter Pan*

Here is a child of <u>three</u> years old, and she cannot tell who made her! Without question, she is equally in the dark as to her soul, its present depravity, and future destiny!

Nathaniel Hawthorne,
The Scarlet Letter

I was fond of the world at that
age. Magic happened. When an
adult explained the concept
of hell to me at age <u>four,</u> I dug
a hole in the backyard and
saw naked people dancing
underground.

Amy Tan, *The Opposite of Fate*

5

who are you, little i
(five or six years old)
peering from some high
window; at the gold
of november sunset
(and feeling: that if day
has to become night
this is a beautiful way)

E. E. Cummings,
Complete Poems, # 52

6

The undoubted littluns, those aged about <u>six</u>, led a quite distinct, and at the same time intense, life of their own.... Apart from food and sleep, they found time for play, aimless and trivial, in the white sand by the bright water.

William Golding, *Lord of the Flies*

Childhood is only the beautiful
and happy time in contemplation
and retrospect: to the child
it is full of deep sorrows, the
meaning of which is unknown.
Witness colic and whooping-
cough and dread of ghosts, to
say nothing of hell and Satan,
and an offended Deity in the sky,
who was angry when I wanted
too much plumcake. Then
the sorrows of older persons,
which children see but cannot
understand, are worse than all.
All this to prove that we are
happier than when we were
<u>seven</u> years old.

George Eliot, *letter,*
May 1844

It is still possible, even for
a child <u>eight</u> years old, on
returning from a museum of
natural history, to say to its
mother: "Mamma, I love you
so; if you ever die, I am going
to have you stuffed and set you
up here in the room so I can
always, always see you!" So little
does the childish conception of
being dead resemble our own.

Sigmund Freud,
The Interpretation of Dreams

9

When you are <u>nine</u> years old,
what you remember seems
forever; for you remember
everything and everything is
important and stands big and
full and fills up Time and is so
solid that you can walk around
and around it like a tree and look
at it. You are aware that time
passes, that there is a movement
in time, but that is not what
Time is. Time is not a movement,
a flowing, a wind then, but is,
rather, a kind of climate in which
things are, and when a thing
happens it begins to live and
keeps on living and stands solid
in Time like the tree that you can
walk around.

Robert Penn Warren,
Blackberry Winter

We do not, cannot, know the meanings of all their words, for we are nine and ten years old. So we watch their faces, their hands, their feet, and listen for truth in timbre.

Toni Morrison, *The Bluest Eye*

10

I wasnt but <u>ten</u> year old.
Not old enough to know what
you were doing.

Cormac McCarthy, *Suttree*

11

I seem to remember that
at <u>eleven</u> my brood were
howlers and screamers and
runners in circles.

John Steinbeck, *East of Eden*

12

The son will run away from
the family not at eighteen but
at <u>twelve</u>, emancipated by his
gluttonous precocity; he will fly,
not to seek heroic adventures,
not to deliver a beautiful prisoner
from a tower, not to immortalize
a garret with sublime thoughts,
but to found a business, to enrich
himself and to compete with his
infamous papa.

Charles Baudelaire,
Intimate Journals

13

People don't know what to
make of him, he doesn't know
what to make of himself, he's
only thirteen, *athletically and
socially inept,* not astonishingly
bright, but there are antennae;
he has… some sort of receivers
in his head; things speak to
him, he understands more than
he should, the world winks at
him through its objects, grabs
grinning at his coat. Everybody
else is in on some secret he
doesn't know; they've forgotten
to tell him.

John Barth, *Lost in the Funhouse*

14

Even though I'm only <u>fourteen</u>, I know what I want, I know who's right and who's wrong, I have my own opinions, ideas, and principles, and though it may sound odd coming from a teenager, I feel I'm more of a person than a child — I feel I'm completely independent of others.

Anne Frank,
The Diary of Anne Frank

15

At <u>fifteen</u> life had taught me
undeniably that surrender, in
its place, was as honorable
as resistance, especially if one
had no choice.

Maya Angelou,
I Know Why the Caged Bird Sings

16

At <u>sixteen</u> the adolescent knows what it is to suffer, for he himself has suffered; but he hardly knows that others suffer too.

Jean-Jacques Rousseau, *Emile*

17

No one's serious at <u>seventeen</u>
When lindens line the promenade.

Arthur Rimbaud, *Novel*

18

At eighteen the true narrative of life is yet to be commenced. Before that time we sit listening to a tale, a marvellous fiction; delightful sometimes and sad sometimes; almost always unreal. Before that time our world is heroic; its inhabitants half-divine or semi-demon; its scenes are dream-scenes: darker woods, and stranger hills; brighter skies, more dangerous waters; sweeter flowers, more tempting fruits; wider plains, drearier deserts, sunnier fields than are found in nature, over-spread our enchanted globe....

At eighteen, drawing near the confines of illusive, void dreams, Elf-land lies behind us, the shores of Reality rise in front....

At eighteen we are not aware of this. Hope, when she smiles on us, and promises happiness to-morrow, is implicitly believed; — Love, when he comes wandering like a lost angel to our door, is at once admitted, welcomed, embraced: his quiver is not seen; if his arrows penetrate, their wound is like a thrill of new life: there are no fears of poison, none of the barb which no leech's hand can extract: that perilous passion — an agony ever in some of its phases; with many, an agony throughout — is believed to be an unqualified good: in short, at eighteen the school of Experience is to be entered, and her humbling, crushing, grinding, but yet purifying and invigorating lessons are yet to be learnt.

Charlotte Brontë, *Shirley*

19

When I was <u>nineteen</u>, pureness
was the great issue.

Sylvia Plath, *The Bell Jar*

One knows who one is; in childish egotism, one supposes people have a relationship only with oneself. But after the age of twenty, the frame is uncertain, change is hard to pin down, one is less and less sure of who one is, and other egos with their court of adherents invade one's privacy with theirs.

V. S. Pritchett, *The Midnight Oil*

TWENTY

20

In the usual way of <u>twenty</u>-year-olds,
when home in Philo, I made a point
of arguing with members of my
family about their political attitudes,
and yet then outside the home I often
found myself reflexively holding,
or at least sympathizing with, those
same parental attitudes. I suppose
all this meant was that I hadn't yet
formed a stable identity of my own.

David Foster Wallace, *The Pale King*

21

I have come legally to man's
estate. I have attained the dignity
of twenty-one. But this is a sort
of dignity that may be thrust
upon one. Let me think what I
have achieved.

Charles Dickens, *David Copperfield*

22

"[Room] 43 must be free," said the young man who was sure he would not be killed because he was <u>twenty-two</u> years old.

Marcel Proust,
In Search of Lost Time, Volume VI

23

One of the mixed blessings of
being twenty and twenty-one
and even <u>twenty-three</u> is the
conviction that nothing like
this, all evidence to the contrary
notwithstanding, has ever
happened to anyone before.

Joan Didion, *Goodbye to All That*

24

She was <u>twenty-four</u> years old. She wanted to inhabit facts, not dreams.

Salman Rushdie,
Shalimar the Clown

25

At twenty-five I was dumbfounded afresh
By my ignorance of the simplest things.

Ted Hughes, *Fulbright Scholars*

26

I was <u>twenty-six</u>. I thought: this is maturity. This is civilisation.

Martin Amis, *Experience*

27

Twenty-seven!... It was a time of
sudden revelations. "Heyyyy, know
what? This thought came to me."

Joyce Carol Oates, *Blonde*

28

Physical identity meant a great
deal to me when I was <u>twenty-eight</u>
years old. I had almost the same
kind of relationship with my mirror
that many of my contemporaries
had with their analysts. When I
began to wonder who I was, I took
the simple step of lathering my face
and shaving.

Don DeLillo, *Americana*

29

It sometimes happens that a woman
is handsomer at <u>twenty-nine</u>
than she was ten years before; and,
generally speaking, if there has been
neither ill health nor anxiety, it is
a time of life at which scarcely any
charm is lost.

Jane Austen, *Persuasion*

At thirty a man steps
out of the darkness
and wasteland of
preparation into active
life; it is the time
to show oneself, the
time of fulfillment.

Thomas Mann, *Joseph and his Brothers*

THIRTY

30

<u>Thirty</u> — the promise of a
decade of loneliness, a thinning
list of single men to know, a
thinning brief-case of enthusiasm,
thinning hair.

F. Scott Fitzgerald, *The Great Gatsby*

31

No, life isn't over at the age of
thirty-one, Prince Andre suddenly
decided definitively, immutably.
It's not enough that I know all
that's in me, everyone else must
know it, too.

Leo Tolstoy, *War and Peace*

32

He was not so old — <u>thirty-two</u>.
His temperament might be said
to be just at the point of maturity.

James Joyce, *Dubliners*

33

He was nearly <u>thirty-three</u>. What good was patience? It wasn't time that freed you from traps. It was truth. And he would fight for it. Cunningly and untiringly.

A. B. Yehoshua,
The Liberated Bride

34

For a man to take it at <u>thirty-four</u>
as a guide-book to what life
holds is about as safe as it would
be for a man of the same age
to enter Wall Street direct from
a French convent, equipped
with a complete set of the more
practical Alger books.

Ernest Hemingway,
The Sun Also Rises

35

My age — thirty five — shouted
at me all the time, standing
tall and wide in my head, and
blocking access to what my
life afforded. Thirty-five never
sat down with its hands folded.
Thirty-five had no composure.
It was always humming mean,
terse tunes on a piece of folded
cellophane.

Carol Shields, *Unless*

36

"Thirty-six years old, biological clock buzzing like crazy, and it looked like my last chance for — you know — for real happiness."

Tim O'Brien, *Tomcat in Love*

37

She was thirty-seven or
thirty-eight years of age, he
shrewdly reckoned, and this
meant that she was looking
for a husband. This, in itself,
was not wicked, or even
funny. Simple and general
human conditions prevailed
among the most seemingly
sophisticated.

Saul Bellow, *Herzog*

38

How oddly situated a man is apt
to find himself at age <u>thirty-eight</u>!
His youth belongs to the distant
past. Yet the period of memory
beginning with the end of youth
and extending to the present has
left him not a single vivid
impression. And therefore he
persists in feeling that nothing more
than a fragile barrier separates
him from his youth. He is forever
hearing with the utmost clarity
the sounds of this neighboring
domain, but there is no way to
penetrate the barrier.

Yukio Mishima, *Runaway Horses*

39

At <u>thirty-nine</u>, everybody's
their own problem.

John Updike, *Rabbit Remembered*

Men at forty
Learn to close softly
The doors to rooms they
    will not be
Coming back to.

Donald Justice, *Men at Forty*

FORTY

After the age of <u>forty</u> a man's flat
gives a good indication of what he
is and what he has deserved.

Aleksandr Solzhenitsyn, *Cancer Ward*

When we are <u>forty-one</u> we all
think it would be nice to make a
fresh start. It's the kind of thing
we laugh at when we're forty-two.

V. S. Naipaul, *Guerrillas*

42

I'm <u>forty-two</u> years old — which
is a lot more like middle age than
forty or even forty-one. Neither
old nor young.

Claire Messud, *The Woman Upstairs*

43

According to my dermatologist,
the neck starts to go at <u>forty-three</u>,
and that's that…. short of surgery,
there's not a damn thing you
can do about a neck. Our faces are
lies and our necks are the truth.

Nora Ephron, *I Feel Bad About My Neck*

44

He felt his own age, <u>forty-four</u>,
felt it as if he were finally
one age, not seven, felt as if he
were a solid embodiment of
bone, muscle, heart, mind, and
sentiment to be a man, as if he
had arrived.

Norman Mailer, *Armies of the Night*

45

He was a man of <u>forty-five.</u>
Forty-five! In five more
years fifty. Then sixty — then
seventy — then it was finished.
My God — and one still was
so unestablished!

D. H. Lawrence, *The Rainbow*

46

At 46 one must be a miser; only
have time for essentials.

Virginia Woolf, *The Diary of
Virginia Woolf,* March 22, 1928

47

He was only <u>forty-seven</u>. Too early to contemplate life insurance.

Dave Eggers, *Zeitoun*

48

KING LEAR How old art thou?
KENT Not so young, sir, to love a
woman for singing, nor so old to
dote on her for any thing: I have
years on my back <u>forty-eight</u>.

Shakespeare, *King Lear*

49

Life always *had* gotten better.
There'd always been more to
come. Although, he was <u>forty-nine</u>
now, and there were changes you
didn't notice — physical, mental,
spiritual changes. Parts of life
had been lived and never would
be again. Maybe the balance's
tip had *already* occurred, and
something about *today,* when
he'd later think back from some
point further on, *today* would
seem to suggest that then was
when "things" began going wrong,
or were already wrong, or was
even when "things" were at their
greatest pinnacle.

Richard Ford, *A Multitude of Sins*

Love is lame at fifty years.

Thomas Hardy, *The Revisitation*

FIFTY

When they have reached fifty
years of age, then let those
who still survive and have
distinguished themselves in
every action of their lives,
and in every branch of
knowledge, come at last to their
consummation: the time has
now arrived at which they must
raise the eye of the soul to the
universal light which lightens all
things, and behold the absolute
good; for that is the pattern
according to which they are to
order the State and the lives of
individuals, and the remainder
of their own lives also; making
philosophy their chief pursuit.

Plato, *The Republic*

51

Fifty-one was too old for dreams
of the future. At fifty-one you
had to keep running just to
escape the avalanche of your
own past.

Stephen King, *Needful Things*

52

I picked up coffee in town, but
skipped the doughnuts and
scones; after <u>fifty-two</u> years, my
body owes me nothing.

Amy Hempel,
The Dog of the Marriage

53

I shall be <u>fifty-three</u>.... I
must confess I find it difficult
to become accustomed to
the thought that the yellow leaf
is upon me.

Christopher Isherwood,
Mr. Norris Changes Trains

54

At fifty-four, he thinks a lot of
things, he believes a few, but what
can he really claim to know?

Julian Barnes, *Arthur & George*

55

General Epanchin was in the
very prime of life; that is, about
fifty-five years of age, — the
flowering time of existence, when
real enjoyment of life begins.

Fyodor Dostoevsky, *The Idiot*

56

"You're only <u>fifty-six</u> years old. That's too young to die for money. For principle, for the good of your country, for love, sure. But not for money."

Mario Puzo, *The Last Don*

57

"Fifty-seven; it's a critical age....
Desire is much the same as it ever
was, — but satisfaction brings in its
revenges."

Hjalmar Söderberg, *Doctor Glas*

58

Fifty-eight is the porter's golden age; he is used to his lodge, he and his room fit each other like the shell and the oyster, and "he is known in the neighborhood."

Honoré de Balzac, *Cousin Pons*

59

At <u>fifty-nine</u> a man's indignation
at an insult to his country's honor
is likely to be controlled by the
knowledge that there is nothing
much he can do about it.

John O'Hara, *Ten North Frederick*

Sixty is not a bad age —
unless in perspective, when
no doubt it is contemplated
by the majority of us with
mixed feelings. It is a calm
age; the game is practically
over by then; and standing
aside one begins to remember
with a certain vividness
what a fine fellow one used to
be. I have observed that,
by an amiable attention of
Providence, most people at
sixty begin to take a romantic
view of themselves. Their
very failures exhale a charm
of peculiar potency.

Joseph Conrad, *The Inn of the Two Witches: A Find*

SIXTY

6o

It got harder and harder to
feel indispensable at age <u>sixty</u>.

Tom Wolfe, *A Man in Full*

61

I might, at <u>sixty-one</u> years of age, have been a little inclined to stay at home.

Daniel Defoe, *The Further Adventures of Robinson Crusoe*

62

He was turning <u>sixty-two</u>, not
an age of life-altering shocks but
only of subtle diminishments.

Paul Theroux, *The Lower River*

63

A man must submit to the conditions of humanity, and not quarrel with a cure as incomplete, because in his climacteric year of <u>sixty-three</u>, he cannot recover, entirely, the vivacities of thirty-five.

Thomas De Quincey, *Narrative and Miscellaneous Papers*

64

Sixty-four years old now, inching
ever closer to senior citizenship,
to the days of Medicare and
Social Security benefits, to a time
when more and more of your
friends will have left you.

Paul Auster, *Winter Journal*

65

She found herself at <u>sixty-five</u> telling younger friends that there was nothing to getting old, quite pleasurable really, for if this or that good took itself off, then all kinds of pleasures unsuspected by the young presented themselves, and one often found oneself wondering what the next surprise would be.

Doris Lessing, *Love, Again*

66

At <u>sixty-six</u> I am more rebellious
than I was at 16. Now I *know*
the whole structure must topple,
must be razed.

Henry Miller, *Art and Outrage*

"Fame, success, power, 500 million dollars, world leadership — well, if they should arrive, I might not exactly take to cover, but as for lying awake nights craving them as in my youth I did — well, I really don't care to any more."

Theodore Dreiser, *Life at Sixty-Seven*

68

At sixty-eight a man's not free
to decide whether he shall seem
unapproachable or not. By
that age, the general cast of our
features is set, and the heart,
when it finds that it can no longer
give expression to its feelings,
grows discouraged.

François Mauriac, *Vipers' Tangle*

69

Of me myself — the jocund heart yet
    beating in my breast,
The body wreck'd, old, poor and
    paralyzed — the strange inertia
falling pall-like round me;
The burning fires down in my sluggish
    blood not yet extinct,
The undiminish'd faith —
the groups of loving friends.

Walt Whitman,
A Carol Closing Sixty-Nine

"A man of seventy should know what he wants."

Isaac Bashevis Singer, *The New Year Party*

SEVENTY

70

You must take living so seriously
That even at <u>seventy</u>, for example,
    you'll plant olive trees —
And not for your children, either,
But because although you fear death
    you don't believe it,
Because living, I mean, weighs heavier.

Nâzım Hikmet, *On Living*

71

I was learning at <u>seventy-one</u>
what it is to be deranged. Proving
that self-discovery wasn't over
after all. Proving that the drama
that is associated usually with
the young as they fully begin to
enter life… can also startle and
lay siege to the aged.

Philip Roth, *Exit Ghost*

72

At the age of seventy-two....
he had seriousness — extreme
seriousness — for others, but
never for himself. Tranquillity
was to him.

Herman Melville, *Israel Potter*

73

"He's <u>seventy-three</u>. What's
the sense of risking good money?
Be content."

Jerome Jerome, *Tommy and Co.*

74

"No use, no use, no use! I'm old, old, old! Seventy-four, seventy-four, seventy-four! Oh, Lord! oh, Lord! oh, Lord! Thy ways are past finding out."

Gertrude Franklin Horn Atherton, *A Monarch of a Small Survey*

75

At seventy-five … I am an empty
flagon. Tap me and you will hear
an awful hollow sound. My head
is a tomb quite as empty as the one
Jesus is supposed to have walked
away from.

Gore Vidal, *Julian*

Perhaps in the back of all our
minds is the life expectancy for
our generation. Perhaps this
expectation lingers there alongside
the hours of sleep one should get
or the number of times one is
meant to chew food — eight hours,
twenty chews, and <u>seventy-six</u> years.
We are all heading there and not
to have that birthday is not to have
made it.

Claudia Rankine, *"There is a button
on the remote control called FAV..."*

77

Will I be here at the end of the year? At <u>seventy-seven</u> that is not an irrational question.

P. D. James, *Time to Be in Earnest*

78

Every person <u>seventy-eight</u>
years old lives in a somewhat
depeopled world. The trouble for
me is that I often loved people
much older and wiser than I. So
I'm left now in the lurch, being,
trying to be, the old wise one and
feeling like a great goose.

May Sarton, *Endgame: A Journal
of the Seventy-Ninth Year*

79

— on my <u>seventy-ninth</u> birthday

The way I look
at it, I'm passing through a phase:
gradually I'm changing to a word.
Whatever you choose to claim
of me is always yours;
nothing is truly mine
except my name. I only
borrowed this dust.

Stanley Kunitz, *Passing Through*

To live without models, is that possible at eighty? Relearn astonishment, stop grasping for knowledge, lose the habit of the past, it is too rich, you're drowning in it, look at new people, pay attention to those who can no longer become models for you.

Elias Canetti, *The Secret Heart of the Clock*

EIGHTY

80

I am this day <u>eighty</u> years old:
can I discern between good and
evil? Can thy servant taste
what I eat and what I drink? Can
I hear any more the voice of
singing men and singing women?

Samuel 2, 19:35

At eighty-one years of age he had enough lucidity to realize that he was attached to this world by a few slender threads that could break painlessly with a simple change in position while he slept, and if he did all he could to keep those threads intact, it was because of his terror of not finding God in the darkness of death.

Gabriel García Márquez,
Love in the Time of Cholera

The old Marquis de la Tour-Samuel, who was <u>eighty-two</u>, rose, and, leaning his elbow on the mantelpiece, said in his somewhat shaky voice…. "I am afraid of the dark! But I would not have acknowledged that before I reached my present age. Now I can say anything."

Guy de Maupassant, *The Apparition*

83

And out here, <u>eighty-three</u>, the cortex slack,
Excitatory processes eased to cinders
By Inhibition's tweaking, callused fingers,
Each time my room begins its blur I feel
I've looked in on some city's practice blackout
(Such as must come, should Germany keep on
That road of madness). Each light, winking out. . .

Thomas Pynchon, *Gravity's Rainbow*

84

"Cause what could be more
satisfying than to be able
to go, at the age of eighty-four,
into twenty or thirty different
cities, and pick up a phone, and
be remembered and loved
and helped by so many different
people?"

Arthur Miller, *Death of a Salesman*

85

Skotoma himself, at eighty-five, was inclined to consider his tumultuous past as a preliminary stage far inferior to his present philosophical period, for, not unnaturally, he saw his decline as a ripening and an apotheosis.

Vladimir Nabokov, *Bend Sinister*

86

"What does it feel like to be
eighty-six, Mrs. Threadgoode?"
"Well, I don't feel any different.
Like I say, it just creeps up
on you. One day you're young
and the next day your bosoms
and your chin drops."

Fannie Flagg, *Fried Green Tomatoes
at the Whistle Stop Cafe*

87

He's what, eighty-six, <u>eighty-seven</u>
years old. It's now or never.

Tobias Wolff, *Old School*

88

At eighty-eight he was still organically sound but suffering terribly from the thought that no one ever told him anything.

John Galsworthy, *In Chancery*

89

What is the sound of an eighty-nine-
year-old heart breaking? It might
not be much more than silence, and
certainly a small slight sound.

Sebastian Barry, *On Canaan's Side*

The man of ninety, dying,
carries with him to the
grave, if not the boyhood
illusion of one woman's love,
the senescent illusion of
all women's faithlessness, and
if not the boyhood illusion
of the goodness of Santa
Claus, the senescent illusion
of the goodness of God.

George Jean Nathan, *The World of George Jean Nathan: Essays, Reviews, & Commentary*

90

At my age (at <u>ninety</u>), the postself is real. I think of my after-death reputation almost every day.

Edwin S. Shneidman,
A Commonsense Book of Death

21

She was the sort that
survives — how else do you
live to be <u>ninety-one</u>?

Wallace Stegner, *Angle of Repose*

Aged <u>ninety-two</u>.
The less safety the better the more curls the better,
    the more powder the better,
the more eggs the better.

Gertrude Stein, *One Sentence*

93

"I aint but <u>ninety-three</u>…. I aint
got so much time I kin hurry it."

William Faulkner, *Flags in the Dust*

"I'm <u>ninety-four</u> years old and I never yet had any peace, to speak of. My mind is just a turmoil of regrets. It's not what I did that I regret; it's what I didn't do. Except for the bottle, I always walked the straight and narrow; a family man, a good provider, never cut up, never did ugly, and I regret it."

Joseph Mitchell, *Old Mr. Flood*

95

"I'll die at <u>ninety-five</u>, which
is the same as never dying."

Roberto Bolaño,
2666: A Novel, Volume 1

At the age of <u>ninety-six</u>, no
bond is any longer possible,
all is merely juxtaposition; a
newcomer is in the way.
There is no longer any room;
all habits are acquired.

Victor Hugo, *Les Misérables*

A man of <u>ninety-seven</u>, unless he's a fool… has no message.

Percy Seitlin, *Letter to My Cousin*

I was curious, a sensation
I hadn't felt in some time.
There is not much left to be
curious about when one
is <u>ninety-eight</u> years old.

Kate Morton,
The House at Riverton

Only got so many
retellings in me.
Can't be casting
my old gems in just
anybody's trough.
At <u>ninety-nine</u>,
you got to hold
something back.

Allan Gurganus,
*Oldest Living
Confederate Widow
Tells All*

You hate to tell new stuff
to somebody around
a hundred years old.
They don't like to hear it.

J. D. Salinger, *The Catcher in the Rye*

ONE HUNDRED

I am almost a hundred years old;
waiting for the end, and thinking
about the beginning.

Meg Rosoff, *What I Was*

NUMBERS HAVE NAMES

1 Antique Type
2 Bodoni
3 Bifur
4 Edwardian Script
5 Champion

0 Antique Type
6 Univers
7 Modern no. 216
8 Piccolo
9 Trajan Pro
10 Gill Sans

11 Bodoni
12 Antique Type
13 Antique Type
14 Beton
15 Gill Sans Shadowed

16 Didot
17 Numbers Strasse
18 Manhattan
19 Gill Sans
20 Baskerville

21 Antique Type
22 Snell
23 Fetish
24 Didot
25 Dorchester

26 Ostrich Sans
27 Egyptienne
28 Valencia
29 Kabel
30 Lust Display

31 Benton Modern
32 Eames Century Modern
33 Goudy Old Style
34 Futura Display
35 Aire Roman Pro

36 Futura Display
37 Didot
38 Outage
39 Sail
40 Alpha Slab One

41 Abril
42 Bordeaux
43 Baskerville
44 Gestalt
45 Requiem

46 AW Conqueror Inline
47 Opti Script
48 Futura Display
49 Numbers Strasse
50 Leawood

51. Numbers Strasse
52. Adam Gorry Lights
53. Willow
54. Last Display
55. Bodoni Highlight
56. Excelsior Script
57. Stymie
58. Sail
59. Blackout
60. Fling
61. Bree
62. Ziggurat
63. Baskerville
64. Adam Gorry Intime
65. Schneider
66. Tondu
67. Odeon
68. Clarendon
69. Raleway
70. Ostrich Sans
71. Stymie
72. Bordeaux
73. Modern No. 20
74. Tondu
75. Lobster Two
76. Sail
77. Eames Century Modern
78. Verlag
79. Gotham Rounded
80. Poplar
81. Futura Display
82. Valencia
83. Century
84. Gill Sans
85. Abril Display
86. Numbers Prospekt
87. Hoefler Text
88. Fling
89. Saracen
90. Blackout
91. Gestalt
92. Sail
93. Splendid Quartett
94. Kabel
95. Granara
96. Braggadocio
97. Benton Modern
98. Bodoni
99. Gothic No. 13
100. Custom

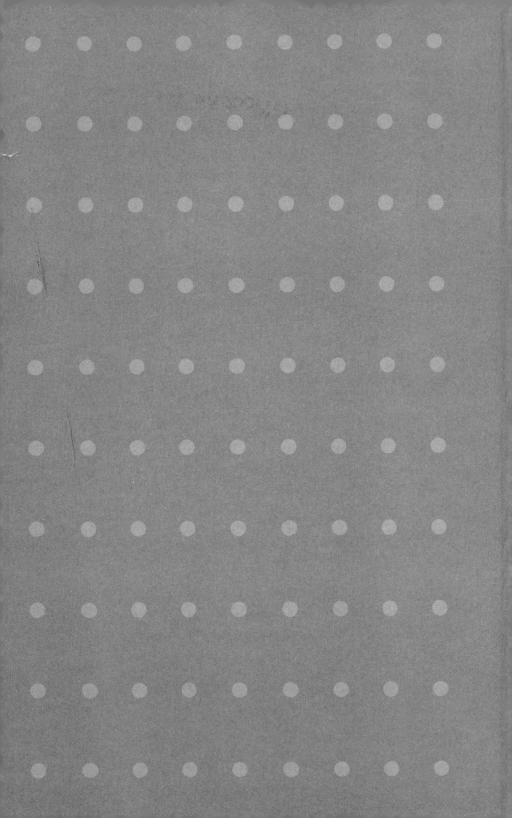